THIS BOOK BELONGS TO:

....

This is a story about a little ghost called Hugo…

Hugo was...

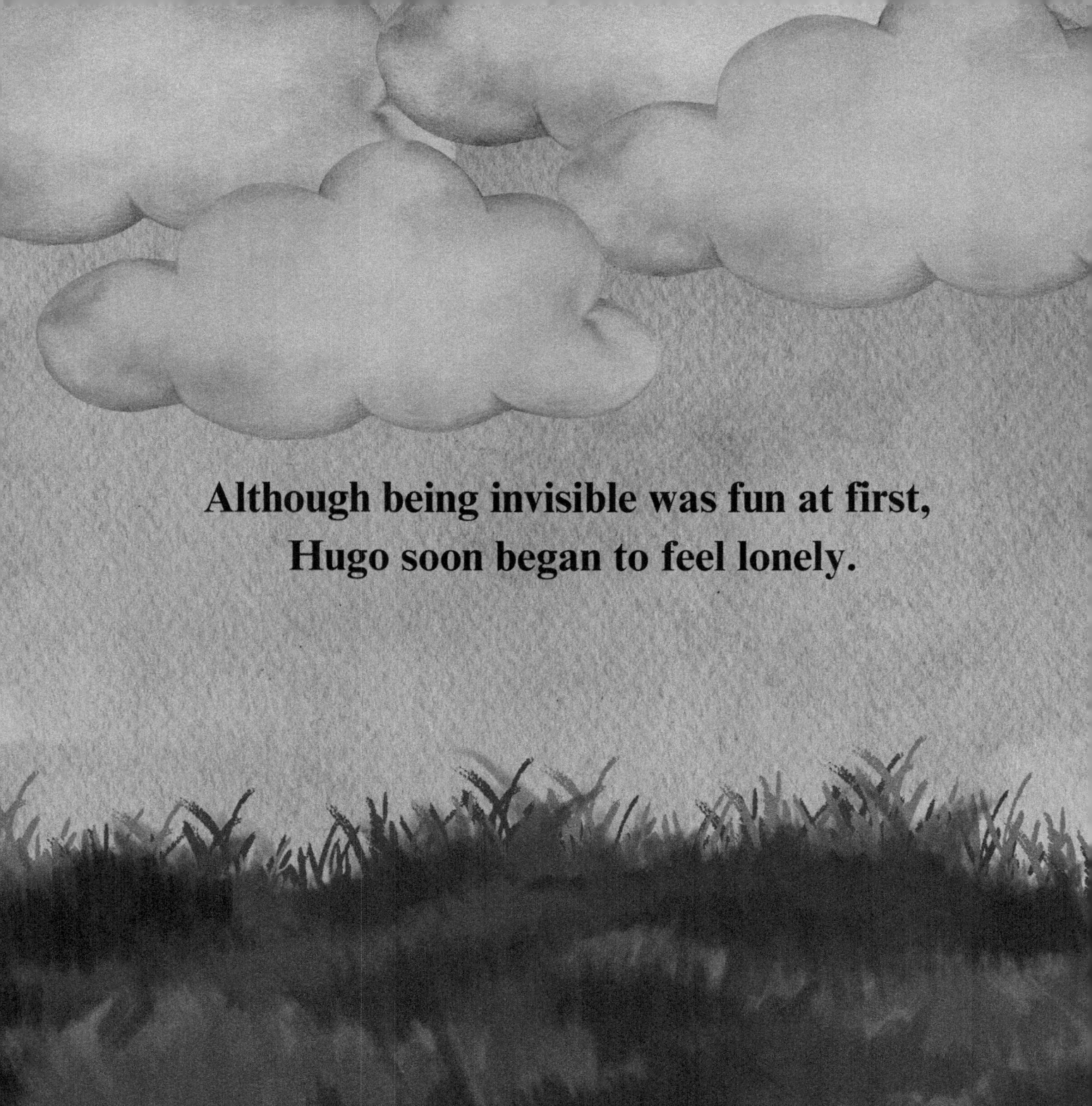

When no one can see you...

It's hard to make friends!

Hugo dreamed of having lots of friends to play with and all of the adventures they would have.

One evening, Hugo went out on a walk.
He stumbled across the most unusual sight!

"Hi, I'm Hugo. what's your name?"

But the ghost couldn't see him...

Hugo was sad, but then he noticed...

They were wearing shoes,
ghosts didn't need to wear shoes!

They were not strange creatures...

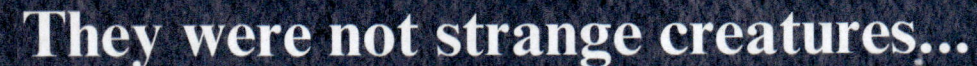

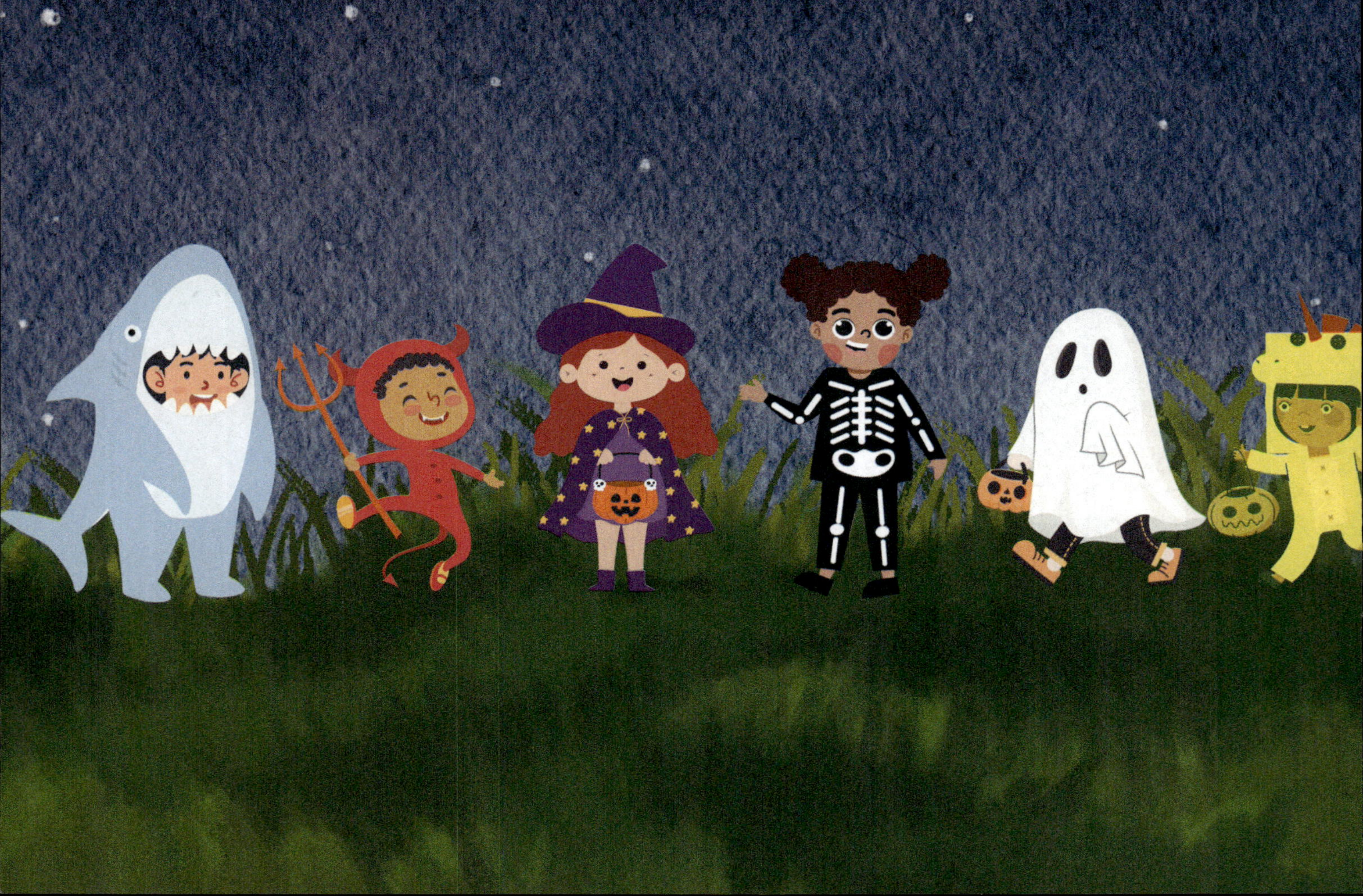

they were children wearing costumes!

Then Hugo had an idea...

a bed sheet.

He tried on lots of

different costumes...

But decided to go as himself.

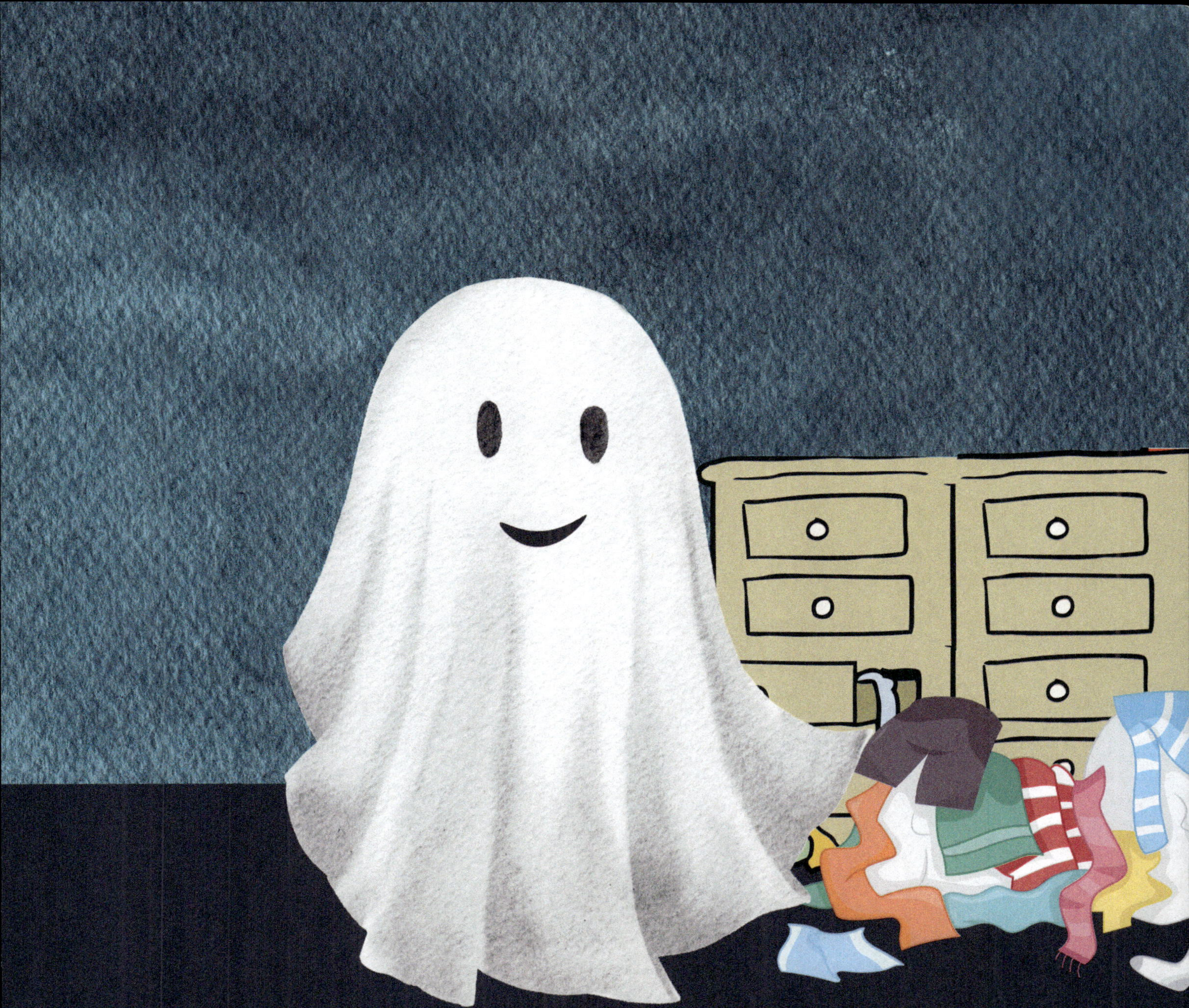

Hugo set off ready for
a big adventure!

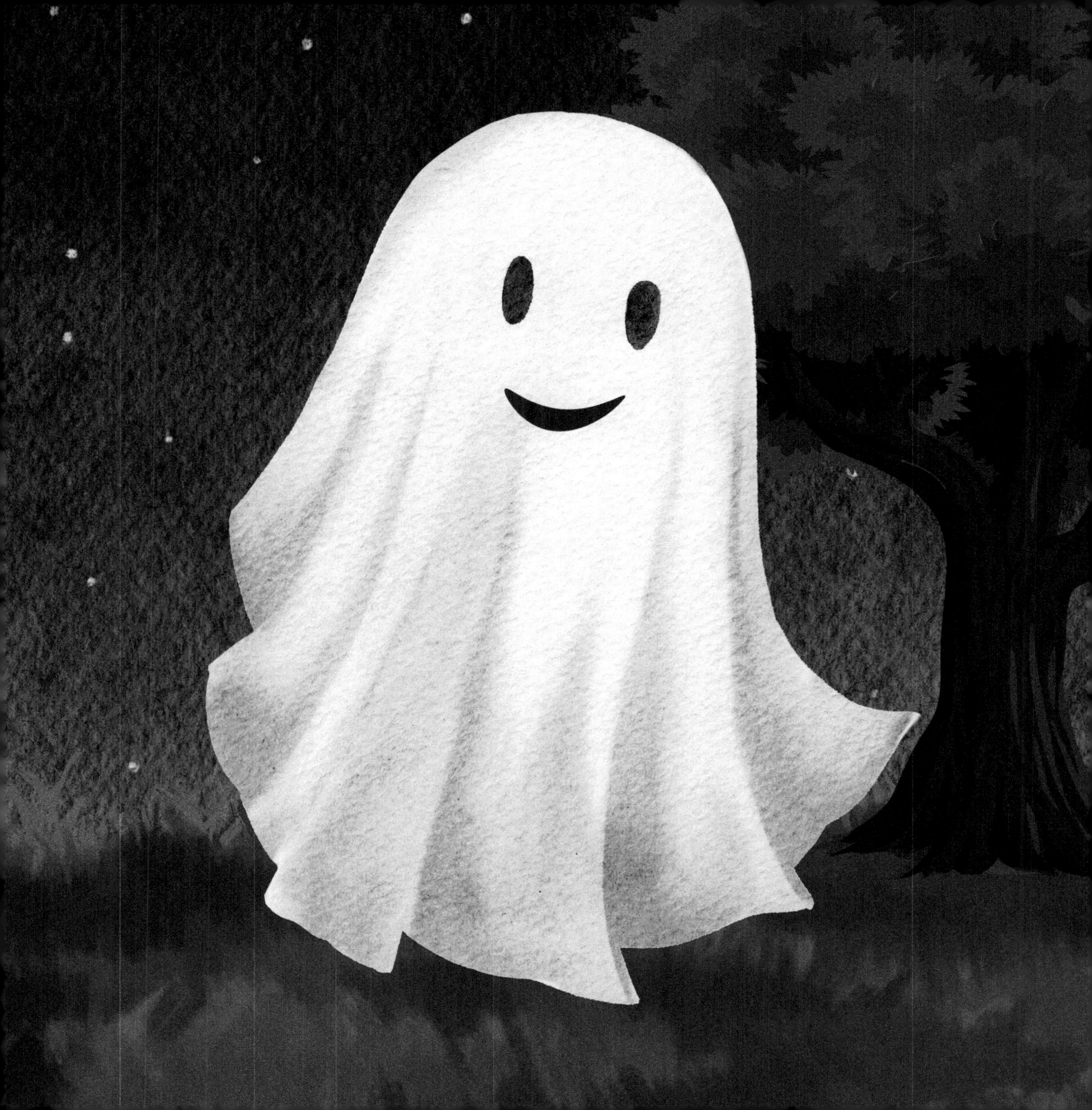

"Hi, I'm Jenna" said the witch,
"I'm Mara" said the skeleton,
"what's your name?"

Hugo was so excited, they could SEE him!

"I'm Hugo," he said,
"would you like to come trick or treating with us?" Jenna asked.

"Yes please!" Hugo replied.

"Everyone come meet Hugo!"
Mara shouted

Everyone rushed over to say hi...

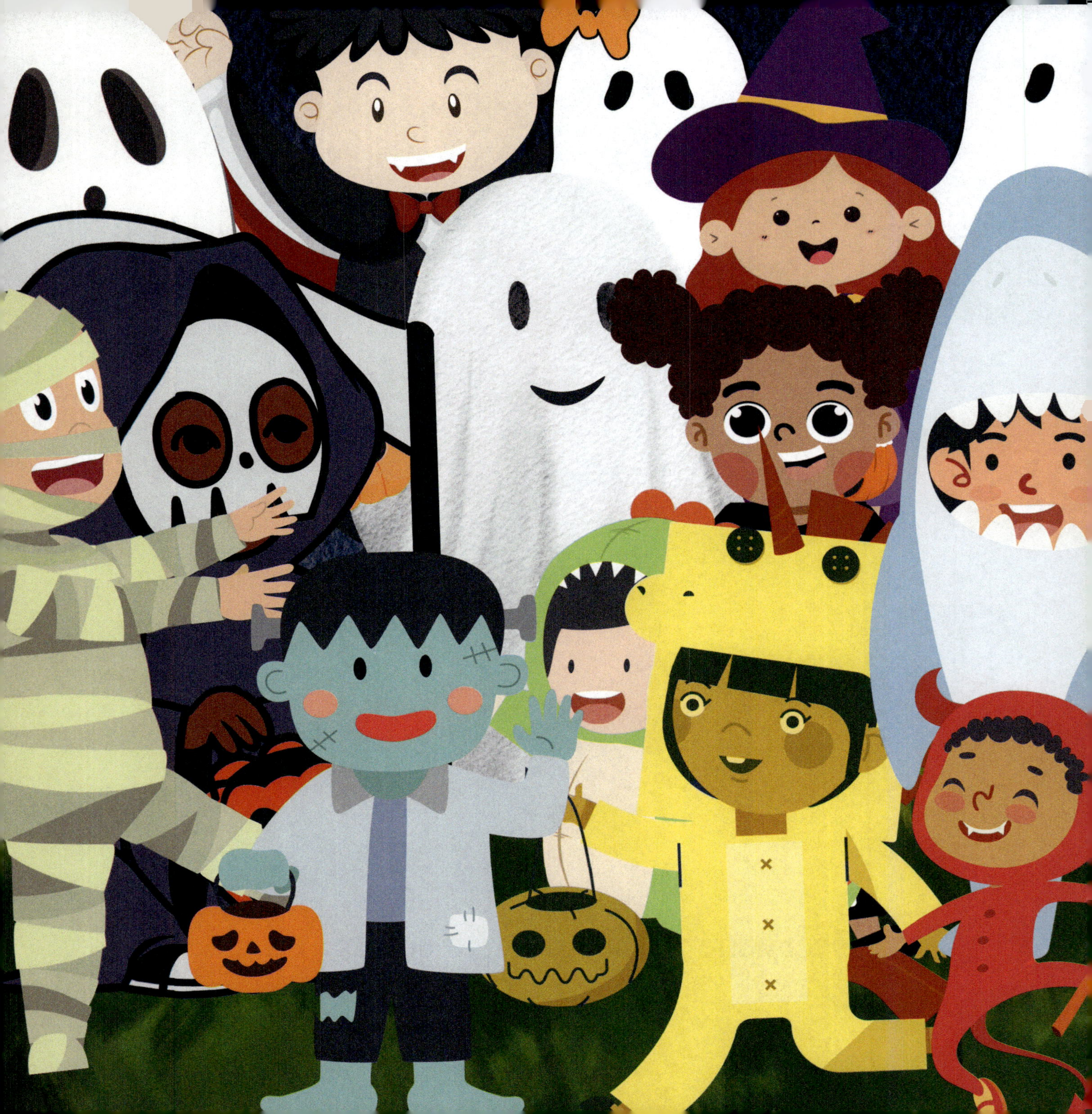

They all jumped back and gasped in shock!

Hugo's bed sheet had fallen off in all the excitement

"You're invisible!" screamed Jenna.
"That' so cool!" one of the children shouted.

"I'm a ghost," said Hugo, putting his costume back on.

"Can you teach us how to be invisible Hugo?
We want to be invisible too!"

"Yes I can!"

Hugo shouted excitedly.

Hugo's guide to making a ghost costume!

Please ask an ADULT for help!

You will need:

1 bed sheet -
big enough to cover you completely

1 marker pen

1 pair of scissors

You can use a wipeable table cloth if you want your costume to be water proof.

Instructions:

1. Collect all of the things you will need.

2. Stand up straight.

3. Ask your adult to put the bedsheet over your head.

4. Make sure the bedsheet is covering you and is equal all the way around.

5. If your bedsheet is too long, ask your adult to cut it to the right length.

6. While still wearing your bed sheet, ask your adult to draw big circles around your eyes with the marker.

7. You can also ask them to draw around the tip of your nose and your mouth and shoulders for arms holes too, but its not essential!

8. Take off your bed sheet.

9. Using the scissors cut out the eye holes and nose, mouth and arms too if you added them.

You may need help from your adult to do this.

10. Put your bed sheet back over your head.

TADA!
You are now an invisible ghost just like Hugo.

Make your costume your own by adding accessories!

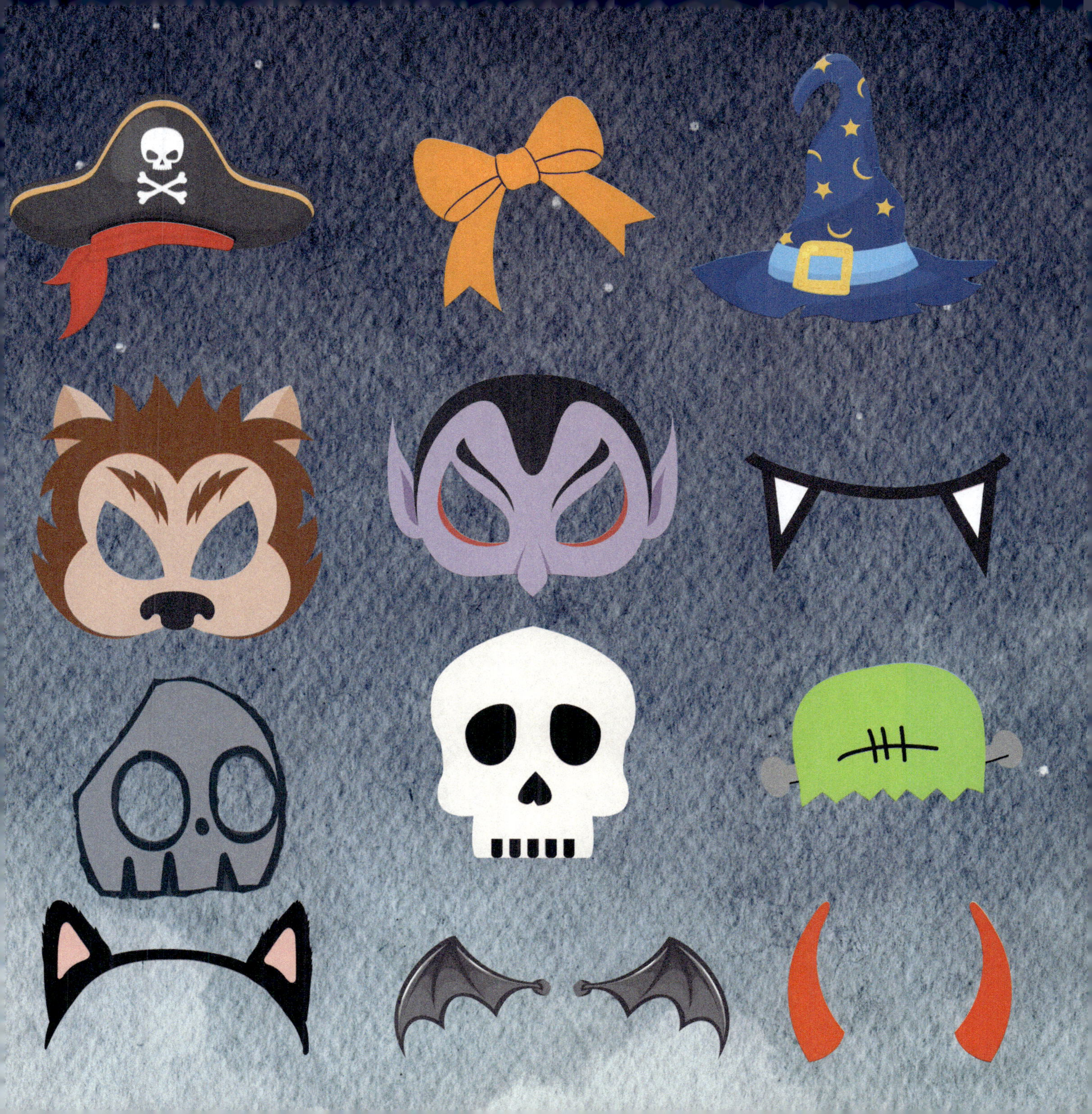

Everyone followed Hugo's instructions.

"Yay! We're all invisible."
They admired each other's new costumes.

The children played together until it was time to go home...

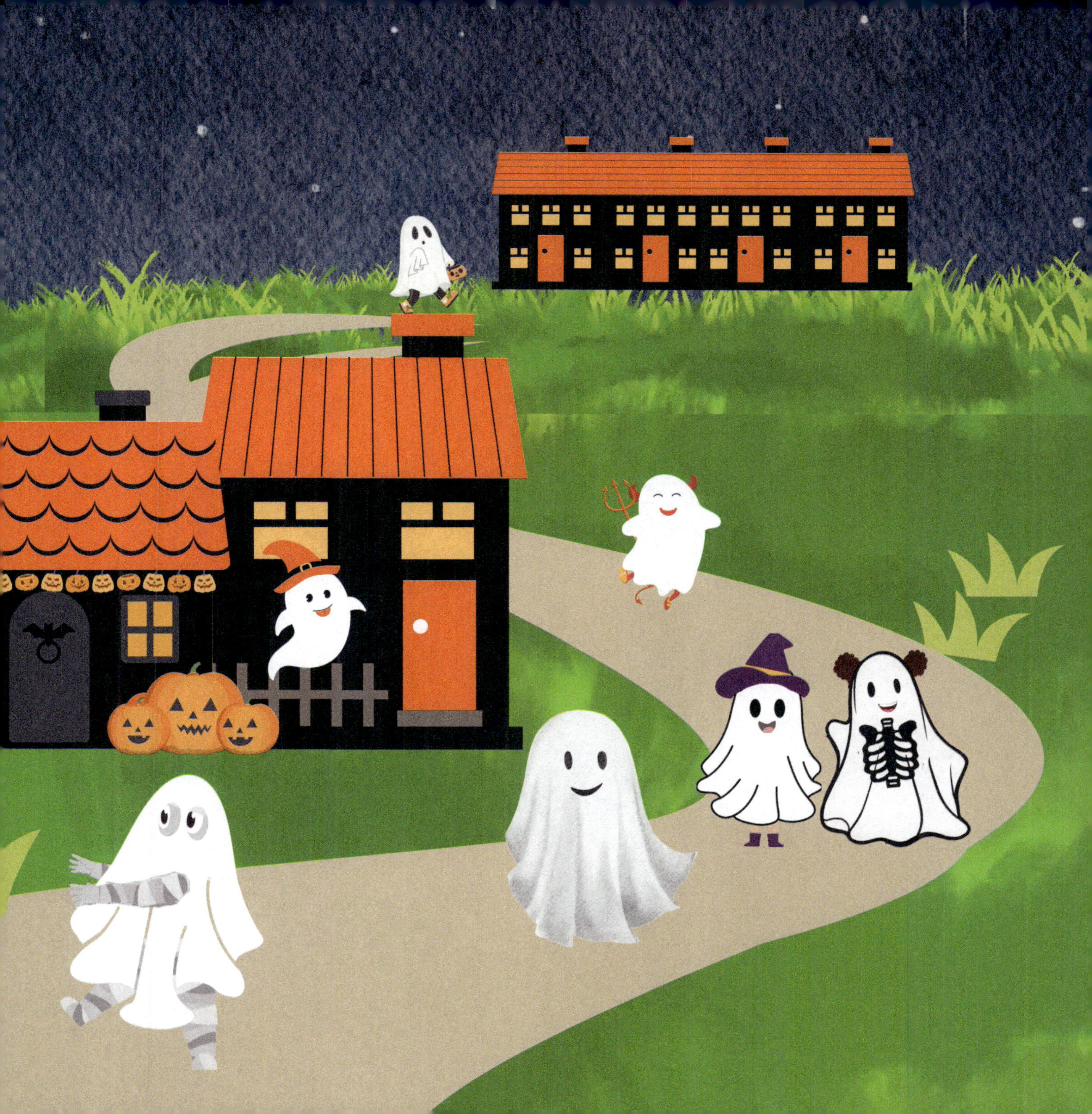

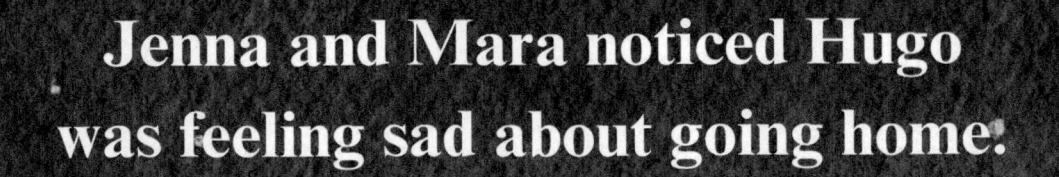

Jenna and Mara noticed Hugo was feeling sad about going home.

They had an idea. "Meet us at the playground tomorrow, wear your ghost costume!"

The next day Hugo
put on his ghost costume…

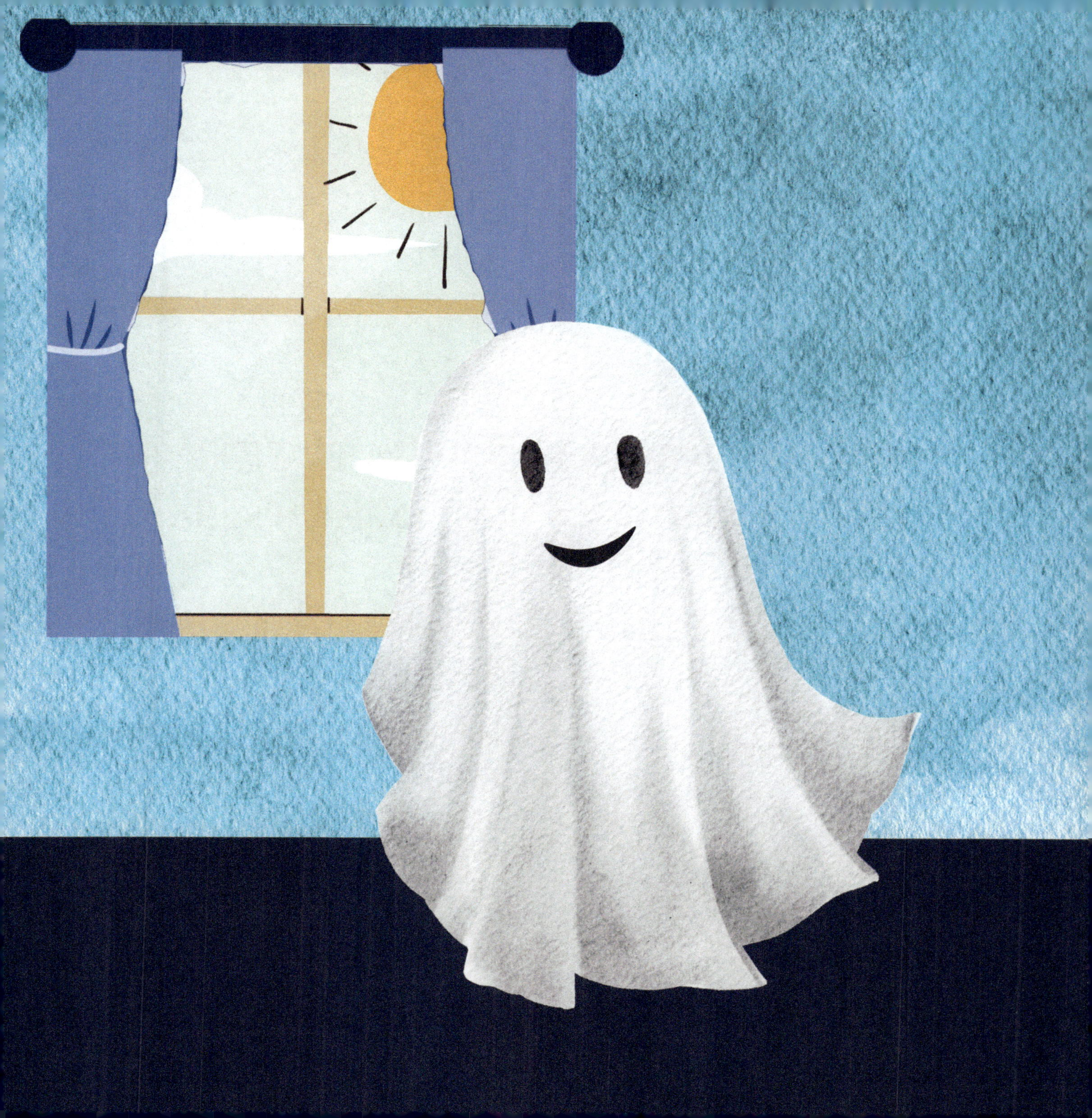

and nervously headed to the playground.
Where he saw the most unusual sight...

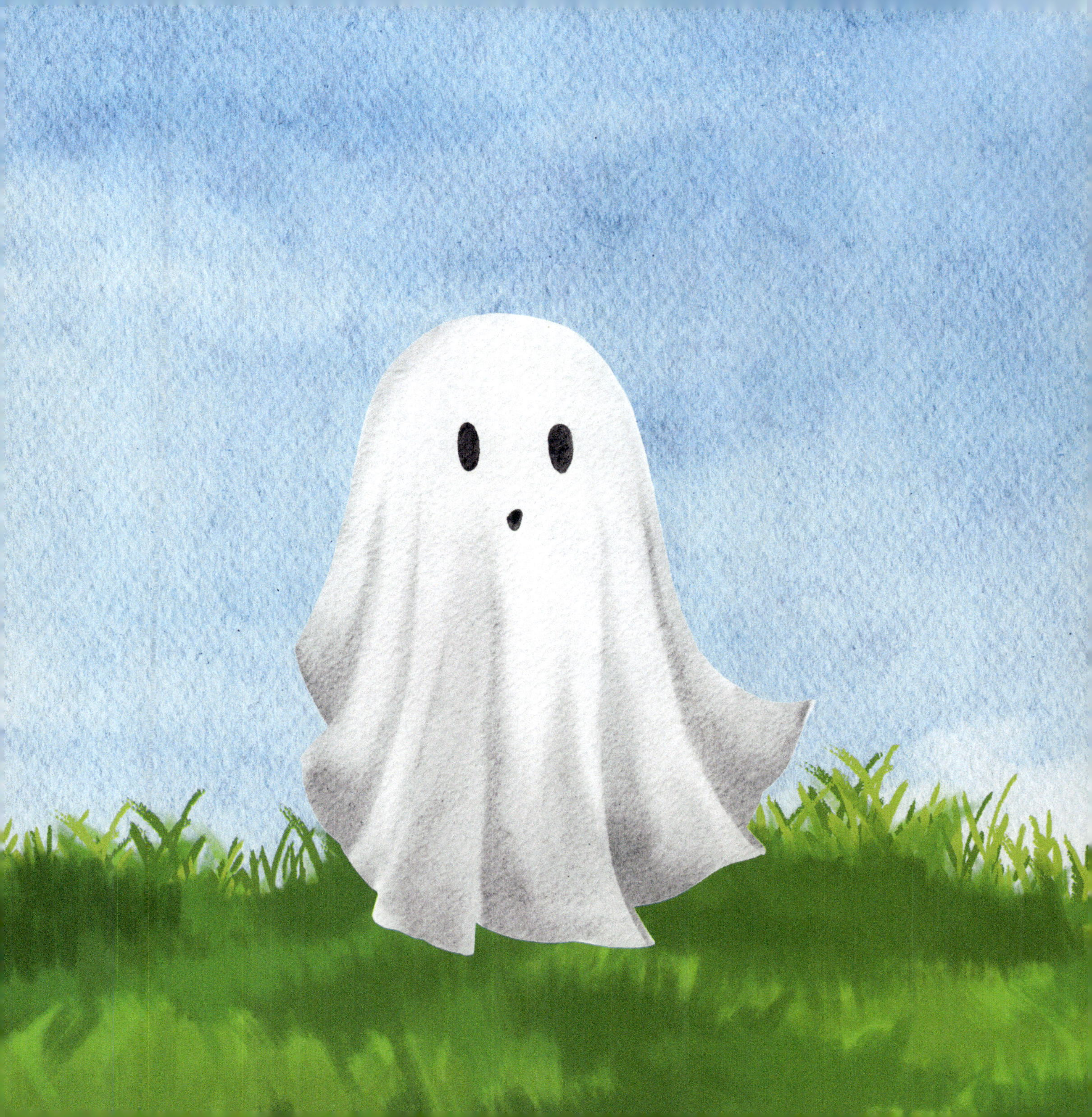

There were the strangest creatures;
pirates, princesses, superheroes, fairies and all sorts of animals.

Hugo took another look around...

They were not strange creatures...

They were his friends wearing costumes!

"We thought you might feel silly being the only one wearing a costume," said Jenna.

"We are going to wear costumes so you can come out and play with us everyday!" said Mara.

Hugo's dream of having friends to play with had come true, he was so happy!

From that day on the children played together every single day!

THE

END

Copyright © 2012
Britney Sewell
All rights reserved.

Printed in Great Britain
by Amazon